Addition and Subtraction

Lucille Caron
Philip M. St. Jacques

Enslow Publishers, Inc.

40 Industrial Road   PO Box 38
Box 398   Aldershot
Berkeley Heights, NJ 07922   Hants GU12 6BP
USA   UK

http://www.enslow.com

Library of Congress Cataloging-in-Publication Data

Caron, Lucille.
      Addition and subtraction / Lucille Caron and Philip M. St. Jacques.
         p. cm. — (Math success)
      Includes bibliographical references and index.
      Summary: Describes the basic principles of adding and subtracting and explains how to
perform these activities.
      ISBN 0-7660-1432-0
      1. Addition—Juvenile literature. 2. Subtraction—Juvenile literature. [1. Addition.
2. Subtraction.] I. St. Jacques, Philip M. II. Title. III. Series.
QA115 .C24 2000
513.2'11—dc21

                                          99-039205

Printed in the United States of America

10 9 8 7 6 5

To Our Readers: We have done our best to make sure all Internet addresses in this book were active and appropriate when we went to press. However, the author and the publisher have no control over and assume no liability for the material available on those Internet sites or on other Web sites they may link to. Any comments or suggestions can be sent by e-mail to comments@enslow.com or to the address on the back cover.

Cover Illustration: © Corel Corporation (background).

Contents

Subtraction

Introduction

If you were to look up the meaning of the word *mathematics*, you would find that it is the study of numbers, quantities, and shapes, and how they relate to each other.

Mathematics is important to all world cultures, including our world of work. The following are just some of the ways in which studying math will help you:

- ▶ You will know how much money you are spending at the store.
- ▶ You will know if the cashier has given you the right change.
- ▶ You will know how to use measurements to build things.
- ▶ Your science classes will be easier and more interesting.
- ▶ You will understand music on a whole new level.
- ▶ You will be empowered to qualify for and land a rewarding job.

Addition and subtraction are important parts of life. Test grades and stock market changes are calculated using them, as well as batting averages and other sports statistics, baker's ingredients, and chemical formulas. You don't usually go through a day without needing to add or subtract something. Addition and subtraction are also the building blocks for more advanced math.

This book has been written so that you can learn about addition and subtraction at your own speed. You can use this book on your own, or work together with a friend, tutor, or parent.

Good luck and have fun!

1. Adding One-Digit Numbers

One-digit numbers are all around you. They are the basis of any number system.

One-digit numbers include the following whole numbers:

0, 1, 2, 3, 4, 5, 6, 7, 8, 9

The next whole number, 10, represents a group of ten ones. Once you learn how to add one-digit numbers and how to regroup them, adding larger numbers will be a snap.

Adding One-Digit Numbers without Regrouping

One-digit addition without regrouping will give you a sum that is less than ten. Here are all the one-digit numbers whose sums are less than ten.

1	2	3	4	5	6	7	8	9
+ 0	+ 0	+ 0	+ 0	+ 0	+ 0	+ 0	+ 0	+ 0
1	2	3	4	5	6	7	8	9

1	2	3	4	5	6	7	8	2
+ 1	+ 1	+ 1	+ 1	+ 1	+ 1	+ 1	+ 1	+ 2
2	3	4	5	6	7	8	9	4

3	4	5	6	7	3	3	4	3	4	3
+ 2	+ 2	+ 2	+ 2	+ 2	+ 3	+ 4	+ 4	+ 5	+ 5	+ 6
5	6	7	8	9	6	7	8	8	9	9

The sum of 4 + 5 is the same as the sum of 5 + 4.

4 + 5 = 9 and 5 + 4 = 9

whole numbers—Zero and the counting numbers:
0, 1, 2, 3, 4, 5, 6, 7, 8, . . .

Adding One-Digit Numbers with Regrouping

When do you regroup? You regroup when there are ten or more ones. Ten ones are regrouped for 1 ten.

6 ones + 5 ones = 11 ones

□□□□□□ + □□□□□ = □□□□□□□□□□ □

11 ones are regrouped for 1 ten and 1 one.

6 + 5 = 1 ten 1 one

Here are all the one-digit numbers whose sums are ten or greater.

1	2	2	3	3	3	4	4	4
+ 9	+ 8	+ 9	+ 7	+ 8	+ 9	+ 6	+ 7	+ 8
10	10	11	10	11	12	10	11	12

4	5	5	5	5	5	6	6	6
+ 9	+ 5	+ 6	+ 7	+ 8	+ 9	+ 6	+ 7	+ 8
13	10	11	12	13	14	12	13	14

6	7	7	7	8	8	9
+ 9	+ 7	+ 8	+ 9	+ 8	+ 9	+ 9
15	14	15	16	16	17	18

The sum of 6 + 5 is the same as the sum of 5 + 6.

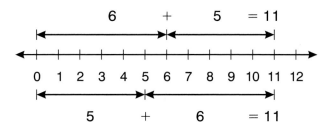

Memorize the basic addition facts with a family member. If you know the basic fact 6 + 7, you also know 7 + 6!

The sum of 6 + 5 is the same as the sum of 5 + 6. This property of addition, called the **commutative property**, will be discussed in Chapter 7.

7

2. Column Addition

Column addition is the addition of three or more numbers. You use column addition when you go shopping, add test grades, or find the number of inches of rainfall for a given month, season, or year.

Column Addition without Regrouping

Suppose you are a meteorologist (weather forecaster) and you have to keep track of the rainfall for one week. It rained 2 inches on Monday, 3 inches on Wednesday, and 4 inches on Saturday. What was the total rainfall for the week?

The order in which these numbers are added will not change the answer, or sum. The numbers to be added are called addends.

Add 2 + 3 + 4

In column addition, arrange the numbers that you are going to add underneath each other, in a column.

Step 1: Add the first two numbers.

$$\begin{array}{r} 2 \\ + 3 \\ \hline 5 \end{array}$$ addend
addend
sum

Step 2: Add the answer in step 1 to the third number.

$$\begin{array}{r} 5 \\ + 4 \\ \hline 9 \end{array}$$ addend
sum

The total rainfall for the week was 9 inches.

---

addend—The number being added in an addition problem.
sum—The answer in an addition problem.

Column Addition with Regrouping

Column addition with regrouping is the addition of three or more numbers with sums of ten or more. When there are ten or more ones, exchange or regroup 10 ones for one ten.

Let's review place value for the number 5,678.

thousands		hundreds		tens		ones
5		6		7		8
5,000	+	600	+	70	+	8

Suppose you had 8 CDs; your friend gave you 9 more, and then you bought 6 more. How many CDs do you have?

You can use column addition and place value to find how many CDs you have in all.

Add 8 + 9 + 6

Step 1: Add the first two numbers.

$$\begin{array}{r} 8 \\ + 9 \\ \hline 17 \end{array} \quad \begin{array}{l} \text{addend} \\ \text{addend} \\ \text{sum} \end{array}$$

Step 2: Add the answer in Step 1 to the third number. Add the ones $(7 + 6 = 13)$. Record 1 ten 3 ones.

$$\begin{array}{r} {}^{1}17 \\ + 6 \\ \hline 3 \end{array}$$

Step 3: Add tens (1 ten + 1 ten = 2 tens). Record 2 tens.

$$\begin{array}{r} {}^{1}17 \\ + 6 \\ \hline 23 \end{array}$$

You have a total of 23 CDs.

In **column addition,** arrange the addends underneath each other, in a column.

3. Adding Two-Digit Numbers

Accountants add two-digit numbers every day. They keep accounts for companies, public offices, and private households. An accountant was given the responsibility to add the following two-digit numbers: 56 and 31. Here is how to find the sum for the accountant.

Adding Two-Digit Numbers without Regrouping

When adding two-digit numbers, first add the numbers in the ones column. Then add the numbers in the tens column. Addition is always done from right to left, beginning in the ones column.

Add 56 + 31

Step 1: Add ones.
Record 7 ones.

```
      ones
     5|6
   + 3|1
      |7
```

Step 2: Add tens.
Record 8 tens.

```
  tens
   5|6    addend
 + 3|1    addend
   8|7    sum
```

The addends are 56 and 31. The sum of 56 and 31 is 87. You did not have to regroup, since the ones column did not add up to more than 9.

You can write the problem using an addition sentence:

$$56 + 31 = 87$$

Two-digit numbers include all the whole numbers from 10 through 99.

Adding Two-Digit Numbers with Regrouping

Add the numbers in the ones column. When there are ten or more ones, use regrouping. Exchange 10 ones for 1 ten and regroup ones.

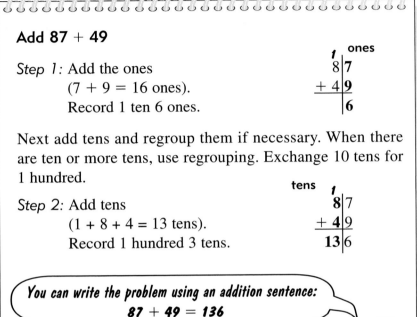

Add 87 + 49

Step 1: Add the ones
(7 + 9 = 16 ones).
Record 1 ten 6 ones.

```
      ones
    1
    8 7
 +  4 9
    ___
      6
```

Next add tens and regroup them if necessary. When there are ten or more tens, use regrouping. Exchange 10 tens for 1 hundred.

Step 2: Add tens
(1 + 8 + 4 = 13 tens).
Record 1 hundred 3 tens.

```
tens   1
       8 7
    +  4 9
       ____
     13 6
```

You can write the problem using an addition sentence:
87 + 49 = 136

Find the added pairs that name the same number:

2 tens + 14 ones	4 tens + 6 ones
1 ten + 15 ones	3 tens + 4 ones
3 tens + 16 ones	2 tens + 5 ones

Make up your own matching pairs, scramble them, and ask a friend or family member to match them up again.

In **column addition**, always add numbers from right to left, beginning in the ones column.

4. Adding Three-Digit Numbers

Adding Three-Digit Numbers without Regrouping

When adding three-digit numbers without regrouping, first add the ones column. Next add the tens column. Finally add the hundreds column. Remember to always add from right to left, recording each column sum until all the addition is complete.

Add 543 + 136

	hundreds	tens	ones	
Step 1: Add ones.	5	4	**3**	
	+ 1	3	**6**	
			9	9 ones (say nine)

	hundreds	tens	ones	
Step 2: Add tens.	5	**4**	3	
	+ 1	**3**	6	
		7	9	7 tens 9 ones (say seventy-nine)

	hundreds	tens	ones	
Step 3: Add hundreds.	**5**	4	3	
	+ 1	3	6	
	6	7	9	(say six hundred seventy-nine)

You can write the equation using an addition sentence:

$$543 + 136 = 679$$

Three-digit numbers are all whole numbers from 100 through 999.

Adding Three-Digit Numbers with Regrouping

Remember that regrouping occurs when a column sum is greater than 9. When a column sum is regrouped, that number must be added to the column on its immediate left.

Add 758 + 467

Step 1: Add ones (8 + 7 = 15 ones).
    Record 1 ten 5 ones.

$$\begin{array}{r} 1 \\ 758 \\ +\ 467 \\ \hline 5 \end{array}$$

Step 2: Add tens (1 + 5 + 6 = 12 tens).
    Record 1 hundred 2 tens.

$$\begin{array}{r} 1\ 1 \\ 758 \\ +\ 467 \\ \hline 25 \end{array}$$

Step 3: Add hundreds
    (1 + 7 + 4 = 12 hundreds).
    Record 1 thousand 2 hundreds.

$$\begin{array}{r} 1\ 1 \\ 758 \\ +\ 467 \\ \hline 1225 \end{array}$$

You can write the equation using an addition sentence:
758 + 467 = 1225

Look through newspapers and magazines for three-digit numbers. Make a collage of all the numbers you find and practice adding any two of these three-digit numbers.

5. Adding Greater Numbers

We can add greater numbers using place value and partial sums. Greater numbers consist of whole numbers that have four or more digits, such as 1,542; 59,871; and 990,245. You can add two four-digit numbers using place value.

Adding Greater Numbers Using Place Value

Basic Fact: 4 + 1 = 5

By putting a zero to the right of each number, you now have:

$$40 + 10 = 50, \text{ or } 4 \text{ tens} + 1 \text{ ten} = 5 \text{ tens}$$

Five tens is the same as fifty.

Basic Fact: 1 + 6 = 7

By attaching three zeros to the right of each number, you now have:

$$1,000 + 6,000 = 7,000, \text{ or}$$
$$1 \text{ thousand} + 6 \text{ thousands} = 7 \text{ thousands}$$

Add 1,542 + 6,315 using place value.

Step 1: Write the value.

1,542 =	1 thousand	5 hundreds	4 tens	2 ones
+ 6,315 =	+ 6 thousands	3 hundreds	1 ten	5 ones

Step 2: Add.

1,542 =	1 thousand	5 hundreds	4 tens	2 ones
+ 6,315 =	+ 6 thousands	3 hundreds	1 ten	5 ones
	7 thousands	8 hundreds	5 tens	7 ones

Step 3: Write the sum.   7,857

You can write the equation using an addition sentence:

$$1,542 + 6,315 = 7,857$$

Use a **comma** in the number when there are four or more digits, such as 7,857. The comma goes between the hundreds and thousands places.

Adding Greater Numbers Using Partial Sums

Partial sums is another method used when adding greater numbers. Partial sums uses place value to find the sum of two or more numbers.

To add 28,634 and 57,918 by partial sums, first list the place value of each digit.

ten thousands	thousands	hundreds	tens	ones
20,000	8,000	600	30	4
50,000	7,000	900	10	8

Add 28,634 + 57,918

Step 1: Add ones.

$$\begin{array}{r} 4 \\ +\ 8 \\ \hline 12 \end{array}$$

Step 2: Add the partial sum 12 to the sum of tens.

$$\begin{array}{r} 12 \\ 30 \\ +\ 10 \\ \hline 52 \end{array}$$

Step 3: Add the partial sum 52 to the sum of hundreds.

$$\begin{array}{r} 52 \\ 600 \\ +\ 900 \\ \hline 1,552 \end{array}$$

Step 4: Add the partial sum 1,552 to the sum of thousands.

$$\begin{array}{r} 1,552 \\ 8,000 \\ +\ 7,000 \\ \hline 16,552 \end{array}$$

Step 5: Add 16,552 to the sum of ten thousands.

$$\begin{array}{r} 16,552 \\ 20,000 \\ +\ 50,000 \\ \hline 86,552 \end{array}$$

$$28,634 + 57,918 = 86,552$$

When you add partial sums, you add the ones. Then you add your answer to the tens, hundreds, thousands, etc.

6. Estimating Sums

An estimation is an educated guess. You use estimations every day. You estimate money, time, and distance. An estimate tells "about how many" or "about how much."

Estimation of whole numbers can be used in addition when an exact value is not needed. Review the basic concept of rounding before you estimate sums.

Rounding

Round 489 to the greatest place value position.

Step 1: What is the greatest place value of the number? (*the hundreds place*)
Underline the greatest place value: 489

Step 2: What digit is to the right of the underlined digit? (8)
Is the digit to the right of the underlined digit five or greater? (*yes*)
If the digit is 5 or greater, add one to the underlined digit (4 + 1 = 5) and replace all the digits to the right of the underlined digit with zeros (*500*).

Step 3: Is the digit four or less? (*no*) If the digit to the right of the underlined digit had been less than 5, the underlined digit would remain the same, and you would replace all digits to the right of the underlined digit with zeros.

489 rounds up to 500

round number—A number written in terms of the nearest whole number, or nearest ten, hundred, tenth, etc.

Estimating Sums to the Greatest Place Value

You can use a number line to round numbers.

Round 7,831 to the greatest number.

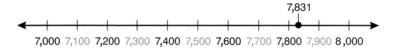

```
                                              7,831
                                                |
←——+———+———+———+———+———+———+———+———●——+———+——→
  7,000 7,100 7,200 7,300 7,400 7,500 7,600 7,700 7,800 7,900 8,000
```

Step 1: Place 7,831 on the number line.

Step 2: Is 7,831 closer to 7,000 or 8,000? *(8,000)*

Step 3: 7,831 rounds to 8,000.

Sums can be estimated to the nearest tens, hundreds, thousands, ten thousands, or higher. When both addends have the same place value, round them to the greatest place value. Then you can find the estimated sum.

Find the estimated sum of 7,831 + 2,345

Step 1: What is the greatest number to which you can round each number?
(thousands place)

Step 2: Round each number to   7,831 rounds to 8,000
the thousands place.   2,345 rounds to 2,000

Step 3: Find the estimated sum.
$$\begin{array}{r} 8,000 \\ +\ 2,000 \\ \hline 10,000 \end{array}$$

The estimated sum of 7,831 + 2,345 is 10,000.

Use a supermarket advertisement to find the prices of the items on your parent's grocery list. Estimate the total cost.

addend—The number being added.
sum—The answer in an addition problem.

7. Addition Properties

You can use the basic addition properties to solve problems. There are three basic addition properties:

1. Commutative Property
2. Associative Property
3. Zero Property

Commutative Property

The commutative property of addition means that, when adding any two numbers, the order in which you add them does not change the sum. You can remember the name by thinking about people who commute to work. When they commute, they change places.

Is the sum of 10 + 30 the same as the sum of 30 + 10?

Add: 10 + 30

$$\begin{array}{r} 10 \\ + 30 \\ \hline 40 \end{array}$$

Add: 30 + 10

$$\begin{array}{r} 30 \\ + 10 \\ \hline 40 \end{array}$$

The sums are the same. So, order is not important when adding two numbers.

Associative Property

The associative property of addition means that when adding three or more numbers, the way in which the numbers are grouped, or associated, does not affect the sum. You can try this with the problem on the following page.

In the **commutative property**, addends may **change places**. In the **associative property**, addends may **associate** in groups.

Your best friend loves to eat fruit. In one week he ate 5 pears, 6 peaches, and 4 apples. How many pieces of fruit did your best friend eat that week?

Add: 5 + 6 + 4

You can group these numbers in two different ways. You can place parentheses around the first two numbers:

$$(5 + 6) + 4$$

or you can place the parentheses around the second two numbers:

$$5 + (6 + 4)$$

Always do the work in the parentheses first.

Is the sum of (5 + 6) + 4 the same as the sum of 5 + (6 + 4)?

Add: (5 + 6) + 4   *Add:* 5 + (6 + 4)

     11   + 4   5 +   10

          15   15

The sums are the same. The way in which you group three or more numbers does not affect the sum.

The Zero Property

The zero property of addition means that the sum of any number and zero is always that number.

Add:	3 + 0	3	Add:	57 + 0	57
		+ 0			+ 0
		3			57

When you add any number and zero, the sum will always be the number.

Adding a **zero** to a number does not change the sum. That's what the zero property means.

8. Problem Solving

The world is filled with information. Making sense of the information is a skill that you need as a regular part of life both inside and outside of school.

Missing Information

There will be times when you will need to make reasonable judgments about information. You will need to decide whether a problem can be solved or whether someone is trying to mislead you. Sometimes real-world situations have missing facts. You should learn to recognize when information is missing.

The following problem is missing some of the information that you will need to solve it.

Your best friend bought 3 apples for lunch. He now has 50 cents. How much money did your best friend spend for the apples?

Ask yourself the following questions to figure out when problems are missing information:

1. What information or facts are given? (*Your best friend bought 3 apples; he now has 50 cents.*)
2. What is the missing data or information? (*The cost of each apple, or the amount of money he started with.*)
3. Can you calculate how much he spent for the apples? (*no*)

problem solving—The process of finding an answer to a question.

Extra Information

It is important to be able to tell the difference between important and unimportant information, or data, in a problem. Data may appear in a variety of sources such as newspapers, magazines, and advertisements. Sometimes this information may include extra information that is not important.

The following problem has too much information. Find the data you do not need to solve the problem.

Hot dogs at a concession stand cost $2.00 each. Five boys and eight girls are buying hot dogs at the concession stand. How many children are buying hot dogs?

Ask yourself the following questions to find out when problems have extra information:

1. What facts or information are given? (*cost of a hot dog, number of boys and girls*)

2. What information is needed to solve this problem? (*number of boys and girls*)

3. What information is not needed to solve this problem? (*cost of a hot dog: $2.00*)

4. What operation do you use to solve the problem? (*addition: 5 boys + 8 girls = 13 children*)

Make up problems with missing information and see if a friend or family member can solve them.

9. Adding Time Values

The following units of time are used in everyday situations:

Units of Time

1 minute	=	60 seconds
1 hour	=	60 minutes
1 day	=	24 hours
1 week	=	7 days
1 year	=	52 weeks
1 year	=	12 months
1 year	=	365 days
1 decade	=	10 years
1 century	=	100 years

Adding Time Values without Regrouping

To add measurements of time, add measurements with the same units.

Add 3 hours 40 minutes + 2 hours 10 minutes

Step 1: Add minutes.

$$\begin{array}{r} 3 \text{ hours } \textbf{40 minutes} \\ + 2 \text{ hours } \textbf{10 minutes} \\ \hline \textbf{50 minutes} \end{array}$$

Step 2: Add hours.

$$\begin{array}{r} \textbf{3 hours } 40 \text{ minutes} \\ + \textbf{2 hours } 10 \text{ minutes} \\ \hline \textbf{5 hours } 50 \text{ minutes} \end{array}$$

3 hours 40 minutes + 2 hours 10 minutes = 5 hours 50 minutes

Always add measurements with the **same units**.

minutes + minutes = minutes

hours + hours = hours

Adding Time Values with Regrouping

To add time with regrouping, add measurements of the same units. If the sum of the minutes is sixty or greater, change minutes to hours.

Add 6 hours 35 minutes + 7 hours 50 minutes

Step 1: Add minutes.

$$6 \text{ hours } \mathbf{35 \text{ minutes}}$$
$$+ \ 7 \text{ hours } \underline{\mathbf{50 \text{ minutes}}}$$
$$\mathbf{85 \text{ minutes}}$$

Step 2: Regroup minutes for hours.

60 minutes = 1 hour
85 minutes = 1 hour 25 minutes

Step 3: Note 1 regrouped hour over the hours column.

$$\overset{1}{6} \text{ hours } 35 \text{ minutes}$$
$$+ \ 7 \text{ hours } \underline{50 \text{ minutes}}$$
$$\mathbf{25 \text{ minutes}}$$

Step 4: Add hours.

$$\overset{1}{\mathbf{6}} \textbf{ hours } 35 \text{ minutes}$$
$$+ \ \mathbf{7} \textbf{ hours } \underline{50 \text{ minutes}}$$
$$\mathbf{14} \textbf{ hours } 25 \text{ minutes}$$

6 hours 35 minutes + 7 hours 50 minutes =
14 hours 25 minutes

I get it!

Write out a weekly time schedule that includes the amount of hours and minutes you spend in school, sports activities, on the phone, eating meals, etc. How much time do you spend in each area for one week?

10. Adding Decimals

People have been studying the decimal system for over 2,500 years. Before the decimal system was created, shopkeepers used wooden or metal counters. The decimal system made it easy to do arithmetic with only paper and pencil.

Look at the following number: 16.35

TENS	ONES	Decimal point	TENTHS	HUNDREDTHS
1	6	.	3	5

Values to the left of the decimal point represent whole numbers, and values to the right of the decimal point represent fractions.

The place to the immediate right of a decimal point has the fractional value of tenths, and the place to the right of that has a fractional value of hundredths.

Adding Decimals with the Same Number of Decimal Places

Add 3.9 + 1.7

Step 1: Line up the decimals.

$$\begin{array}{r} 3.9 \\ + 1.7 \\ \hline \end{array}$$

Step 2: Add tenths. Regroup if necessary (16 tenths = 1 one 6 tenths). Place the decimal point in the sum.

$$\begin{array}{r} {\scriptstyle 1} \\ 3.9 \\ + 1.7 \\ \hline .6 \end{array}$$

Step 3: Add ones.

$$\begin{array}{r} {\scriptstyle 1} \\ 3.9 \\ + 1.7 \\ \hline 5.6 \end{array}$$

3.9 + 1.7 = 5.6

Remember: Numbers to the left of the decimal point are **whole numbers**. Numbers to the right of the decimal point are **fractions**.

Adding Decimals with Different Numbers of Decimal Places

When adding decimals with different numbers of decimal places, you can add zeros to the right of the last digit. The zeros are called placeholders. Then each number will have the same number of digits.

Add 4.6 + 2.59

Step 1: Line up the decimals.

$$\begin{array}{r} 4.6 \\ + \ 2.59 \\ \hline \end{array}$$

Step 2: Insert a zero as a placeholder.

$$\begin{array}{r} 4.6\mathbf{0} \\ + \ 2.59 \\ \hline \end{array}$$

Step 3: Add hundredths.

$$\begin{array}{r} 4.6\mathbf{0} \\ + \ 2.5\mathbf{9} \\ \hline \mathbf{9} \end{array}$$

Step 4: Add tenths. Regroup (11 tenths = 1 one 1 tenth). Place the decimal point in the sum.

$$\begin{array}{r} {\scriptstyle 1} \\ 4.\mathbf{6}0 \\ + \ 2.\mathbf{5}9 \\ \hline .\mathbf{19} \end{array}$$

Step 5: Add ones.

$$\begin{array}{r} {\scriptstyle 1} \\ \mathbf{4}.60 \\ + \ \mathbf{2}.59 \\ \hline 7.19 \end{array}$$

$$4.6 + 2.59 = 7.19$$

Make a list of household objects that include measurements with decimals. Remember to check the kitchen cabinets and freezer.

Adding a zero to the right of the last digit in a decimal will not change the value of the decimal. 4.6 is the same as 4.60

11. Adding Monetary Values

Currency—or money—represents monetary value. The ability to add and subtract monetary value is a skill used in many daily situations. You often use coins and paper currency to purchase items you need.

Coins	Value in cents	Value in dollars
1 penny	1¢	$0.01
1 nickel	5¢	$0.05
1 dime	10¢	$0.10
1 quarter	25¢	$0.25
1 half-dollar	50¢	$0.50

A teacher bought a book and gave the cashier 2 half-dollars, 3 quarters, 4 dimes, and 1 nickel. The cashier asked the teacher for three pennies. How much did the book cost?

Step 1: Using addition, figure out the total value for each type of coin.

half-dollars	quarters	dimes	nickels	pennies
$0.50	$0.25	$0.10	$0.05	$0.01
+$0.50	$0.25	$0.10		$0.01
$1.00	+$0.25	$0.10		+$0.01
	$0.75	+$0.10		$0.03
		$0.40		

Step 2: Add hundredths.
Regroup
(13 hundredths =
1 tenth 3 hundredths).

$$
\begin{array}{ll}
\overset{1}{\$1.00} & \text{half dollars} \\
\$0.75 & \text{quarters} \\
\$0.40 & \text{dimes} \\
\$0.05 & \text{nickel} \\
+\$0.03 & \text{pennies} \\
\hline
3 &
\end{array}
$$

Remember: In column addition, line up the decimal points before you begin to add.

Step 3: Add tenths.
Regroup
(12 tenths =
1 one 2 tenths).

$$
\begin{array}{r}
\overset{1\ 1}{} \\
\$1.00 \\
\$0.75 \\
\$0.40 \\
\$0.05 \\
+\,\underline{\$0.03} \\
.23
\end{array}
$$

Step 4: Add ones.

$$
\begin{array}{r}
\overset{1\ 1}{} \\
\$1.00 \\
\$0.75 \\
\$0.40 \\
\$0.05 \\
+\,\underline{\$0.03} \\
\$2.23
\end{array}
$$

The book cost $2.23, or two dollars and twenty-three cents.

The following is a list of paper money, or bills, used in everyday situations:

Bills	Value in dollars
one-dollar	$1.00
five-dollar	$5.00
ten-dollar	$10.00
twenty-dollar	$20.00
fifty-dollar	$50.00
one-hundred-dollar	$100.00

Go to the mall and see how many different things you could buy with a ten-dollar bill. How many could you buy with a twenty-dollar bill? A fifty-dollar bill?

12. Adding Integers

When you first learned to count, you used the set of counting numbers: 1, 2, 3, 4, . . .

If you include a zero in this set, you have the set of whole numbers: 0, 1, 2, 3, 4, . . .

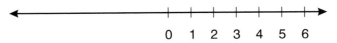

You can expand this set by adding negative numbers to the left of zero on the number line. These are the set of integers.

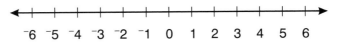

Integers to the right of zero are called positive numbers. Integers to the left of zero are called negative numbers.

Adding Like Integers

Like integers are numbers with the same sign. When adding two integers with like signs, add the numbers as whole numbers. The sum will have the sign of the two integers.

To add two positive numbers, write them with or without the positive sign.

$2 + 5 = 7$, or $^+7$

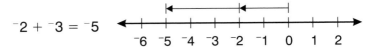

The sum of two or more positive integers is always positive.

You can add two negative numbers:

$^-2 + {}^-3 = {}^-5$

The sum of two or more negative integers is always negative.

---

integers—All the whole numbers and their opposites (negatives).

Adding Unlike Integers

Add 2 + ⁻5

Use white circles to represent positive integers and black circles to represent negative integers.

Step 1: Draw 2 white circles to represent positive two.

Step 2: Draw 5 black circles to represent a negative five.

Step 3: Two black circles are canceled by two white circles. There are 3 black circles left.

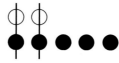

⁻3

Write the answer using an addition sentence: 2 + ⁻5 = ⁻3

When you add a negative number to a positive number, the answer will always be the difference between the two numbers (see page 34 for basic subtraction facts). The sign will be the sign of the greater number. Redo the problem using this rule.

Add 2 + ⁻5

Step 1: Subtract the two numbers.   5 − 2 = 3

Step 2: Compare the two numbers, ignoring the signs.   5 is greater than 2

Step 3: Use the sign of the greater number. The sign of 5 is negative, so the answer is also negative.   2 + ⁻5 = ⁻3

---

like integers—Numbers with the same signs.
unlike integers—Numbers with different signs.

13. Adding Fractions

Fractions are used by carpenters to measure the materials for woodworking projects, by dressmakers to determine the amount of material needed to make a garment, and by cooks to follow recipes. Fractions show the relationship between a part and the whole item.

The numerator is the number at the top of the fraction. It tells you how many parts are being considered. The denominator is the number on the bottom of the fraction. It tells you the total number of parts there are.

$$\frac{\text{numerator}}{\text{denominator}} = \frac{1}{2}$$

Adding Like Fractions

Like fractions are fractions with the same, or common, denominator. For example, $\frac{1}{4}$ and $\frac{3}{4}$ are like fractions because they have a common denominator of 4.

Add $\frac{1}{4} + \frac{3}{4}$

Step 1: Add the numerators and place them over the common denominator.

$$\frac{1 + 3}{4} \quad \text{numerators} \atop \text{denominator}$$

Step 2: Find the sum.

$$\frac{1 + 3}{4} = \frac{4}{4}$$

Step 3: Reduce to lowest terms. $\frac{4}{4}$ is the same as one whole.

$$\frac{4}{4} = 1$$

$$\frac{1}{4} + \frac{3}{4} = 1$$

When fractions have the same denominator, that denominator is called the **common denominator**.

Adding Unlike Fractions

Unlike fractions are fractions that have different denominators.

Add $\frac{1}{2} + \frac{1}{4}$ ■■□□ + ■□□□

$\frac{1}{2}$ + $\frac{1}{4}$

Step 1: Find a common denominator. $\frac{1}{2}$ is the same as $\frac{2}{4}$
(Look at the figure above.)

Step 2: Add the numerators and place $\frac{2}{4} + \frac{1}{4} = \frac{2+1}{4} = \frac{3}{4}$
them over the denominator.

$$\frac{1}{2} + \frac{1}{4} = \frac{3}{4}$$

Add $\frac{1}{2} + \frac{1}{6}$ ■■■□□□ + ■□□□□□

$\frac{1}{2}$ + $\frac{1}{6}$

Step 1: Find a common denominator. $\frac{1}{2}$ is the same as $\frac{3}{6}$

Step 2: Add the numerators and place $\frac{3}{6} + \frac{1}{6} = \frac{3+1}{6} = \frac{4}{6}$
them over the denominator.

Step 3: Reduce to lowest terms. $\frac{4 \div 2}{6 \div 2} = \frac{2}{3}$

$$\frac{1}{2} + \frac{1}{6} = \frac{2}{3}$$

For more details on finding the **least common denominator** of two fractions, see page 59.

14. Adding Mixed Numbers

A mixed number contains two parts: a whole number other than zero and a fraction.

$$6\frac{3}{7} \qquad 2\frac{1}{2} \qquad 8\frac{5}{9}$$

whole number   fraction

Adding Mixed Numbers with Like Denominators

Add $3\frac{4}{9} + 4\frac{1}{9}$

Step 1: Add the numerators and place the sum over the denominator.

$$\frac{4}{9} + \frac{1}{9} = \frac{4+1}{9} = \frac{5}{9}$$

Step 2: Add the whole numbers. $3 + 4 = 7$

$$3\frac{4}{9} + 4\frac{1}{9} = 7\frac{5}{9}$$

Add $1\frac{1}{5} + 3\frac{2}{5}$

Step 1: Add the fractions.

$$\frac{1}{5} + \frac{2}{5} = \frac{3}{5}$$

Step 2: Add the whole numbers.
$$(1 + 3 = 4)$$

$$\begin{aligned} & 1\frac{1}{5} \\ + & 3\frac{2}{5} \\ \hline & 4\frac{3}{5} \end{aligned}$$

$$1\frac{1}{5} + 3\frac{2}{5} = 4\frac{3}{5}$$

A mixed number contains a whole number and a fraction. The following numbers are examples of mixed numbers:

$$2\frac{1}{2} \qquad 4\frac{3}{4} \qquad 5\frac{7}{8}$$

Adding Mixed Numbers with Unlike Denominators

To add mixed numbers with unlike denominators, you need a common denominator.

Add $2\frac{3}{4} + 3\frac{5}{6}$

Step 1: Find the least common multiple (LCM) of 4 and 6.
multiples of 4: 4, 8, **12**, 16, . . .
multiples of 6: 6, **12**, 18, 24, . . .
The LCM is 12.

Step 2: The LCM (12) becomes the least common denominator (LCD). Write the fractions with the LCD.

$$\frac{3}{4} = \frac{3 \times 3}{4 \times 3} = \frac{9}{12}$$

$$\frac{5}{6} = \frac{5 \times 2}{6 \times 2} = \frac{10}{12}$$

Step 3: Add the whole numbers and fractions.

$$2\frac{9}{12} + 3\frac{10}{12} = 5\frac{19}{12}$$

Step 4: Reduce the sum to lowest terms.

$$5\frac{19}{12} = 6\frac{7}{12}$$

least common multiple—The smallest number that appears in the sets of multiples for two numbers.

15. Addition and Subtraction

You use addition and subtraction every day. For example, you may have had a test in math on which you missed four out of the twenty problems. How many problems did you answer correctly?

There were 20 problems on the test, and you answered 4 incorrectly. The number you answered correctly was 16.

You can write this as a number sentence:

$$20 - 4 = 16$$

Inverse Operations

Addition and subtraction are inverse operations. Subtraction has the opposite effect of addition. An inverse operation undoes what another operation does. It is like filling and emptying a glass or tying and untying your shoes.

For example: $8 + 9 = 17$ and $9 + 8 = 17$ are basic addition facts. The corresponding subtraction facts are $17 - 9 = 8$ and $17 - 8 = 9$

Fact Families

If you know that $11 + 7 = 18$, what other facts do you know?

$$7 + 11 = 18 \qquad 18 - 7 = 11 \qquad 18 - 11 = 7$$

If two members of a fact family are 7 and 8, what are possible third members? A possible third member is 15.

$$7 + 8 = 15 \qquad\qquad 8 + 7 = 15$$

$$15 - 8 = 7 \qquad\qquad 15 - 7 = 8$$

operation—A way of combining two numbers.

inverse operation—An operation that undoes what another operation does. Addition and subtraction are inverse operations.

Checking the Sum

Subtraction can be used to check the answer to an addition problem. In addition, you are looking for a sum. In subtraction, you look for a difference, or missing addend.

The answer to an addition problem is correct if the difference between the sum and the addend equals the other addend.

Add 478 + 21

Step 1: Add.

$$\begin{array}{r} 478 \\ +\ 21 \\ \hline 499 \end{array}$$
478 addend
+ 21 addend
499 sum

Step 2: Check by subtracting.
Find the difference of
the sum and the addend.

$$\begin{array}{r} 499 \\ -\ 21 \\ \hline 478 \end{array}$$

Notice, the difference between the sum and the addend is equal to the other addend. The sum is correct.

Checking the Difference

You can use addition to check the answer of a subtraction problem. In subtraction, the first number is called the minuend, and the second is called the subtrahend. The answer is called the difference.

Subtract 647 − 123

Step 1: Subtract.

$$\begin{array}{r} 647 \\ -123 \\ \hline 524 \end{array}$$
647 minuend
−123 subtrahend
524 difference

Step 2: Check by adding.
Find the sum of the
difference and subtrahend.

$$\begin{array}{r} 524 \\ +\ 123 \\ \hline 647 \end{array}$$

Addition: addend + addend = sum
Subtraction: minuend − subtrahend = difference

16. Subtracting One-Digit Numbers

Subtraction is used to compare values or amounts. It can tell you how much greater one number is than another.

Subtraction of one-digit numbers includes basic subtraction facts. Basic subtraction facts include all possible combinations of one-digit whole numbers subtracted from one-digit whole numbers. Here are some of the basic subtraction facts.

When a number is subtracted from itself, the difference is zero.

0	1	2	3	4	5	6	7	8	9
−0	−1	−2	−3	−4	−5	−6	−7	−8	−9
0	0	0	0	0	0	0	0	0	0

When zero is subtracted from a number, the difference is that number.

1	2	3	4	5	6	7	8	9
−0	−0	−0	−0	−0	−0	−0	−0	−0
1	2	3	4	5	6	7	8	9

When a number that is one less than a given number is subtracted, the difference is one.

2	3	4	5	6	7	8	9
−1	−2	−3	−4	−5	−6	−7	−8
1	1	1	1	1	1	1	1

When a number that is two less than a given number is subtracted, the difference is two.

3	4	5	6	7	8	9
−1	−2	−3	−4	−5	−6	−7
2	2	2	2	2	2	2

difference—The answer in a subtraction problem.

When a number that is three less than a given number is subtracted, the difference is three.

$$
\begin{array}{cccccc}
4 & 5 & 6 & 7 & 8 & 9 \\
-1 & -2 & -3 & -4 & -5 & -6 \\
\hline
3 & 3 & 3 & 3 & 3 & 3
\end{array}
$$

When a number that is four less than a given number is subtracted, the difference is four.

$$
\begin{array}{ccccc}
5 & 6 & 7 & 8 & 9 \\
-1 & -2 & -3 & -4 & -5 \\
\hline
4 & 4 & 4 & 4 & 4
\end{array}
$$

When a number that is five less than a given number is subtracted, the difference is five.

$$
\begin{array}{cccc}
6 & 7 & 8 & 9 \\
-1 & -2 & -3 & -4 \\
\hline
5 & 5 & 5 & 5
\end{array}
$$

When a number that is six less than a given number is subtracted, the difference is six.

$$
\begin{array}{ccc}
7 & 8 & 9 \\
-1 & -2 & -3 \\
\hline
6 & 6 & 6
\end{array}
$$

When a number that is seven less than a given number is subtracted, the difference is seven.

$$
\begin{array}{cc}
8 & 9 \\
-1 & -2 \\
\hline
7 & 7
\end{array}
$$

When a number that is eight less than a given number is subtracted, the difference is eight.

$$
\begin{array}{c}
9 \\
-1 \\
\hline
8
\end{array}
$$

Try to memorize the basic subtraction facts.

Basic subtraction facts include all the possible combinations of one-digit numbers subtracted from one-digit numbers.

17. Subtracting Two-Digit Numbers

Two-digit numbers include all the whole numbers from 10 through 99. Subtraction of whole numbers is always done from right to left, beginning in the ones column.

Terms in Subtraction

There are three terms associated with subtraction: minuend, subtrahend, and difference. The minuend is the number from which you subtract. The subtrahend is the number you subtract. The difference is the answer.

The symbol used to indicate subtraction is the minus sign ($-$).

Subtracting Two-Digit Numbers without Regrouping

When subtracting two-digit numbers without regrouping, first subtract the ones column, then subtract the tens column.

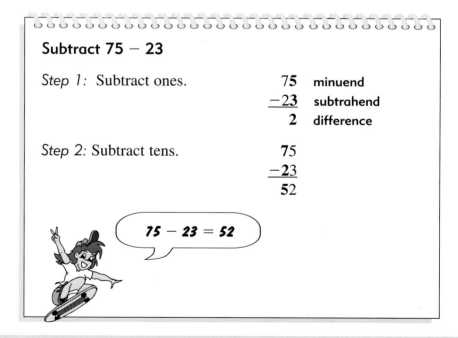

Subtract 75 − 23

Step 1: Subtract ones.

$$\begin{array}{r} 75 \\ -23 \\ \hline 2 \end{array}$$ minuend / subtrahend / difference

Step 2: Subtract tens.

$$\begin{array}{r} 75 \\ -23 \\ \hline 52 \end{array}$$

75 − 23 = 52

minuend—The number from which you subtract.
subtrahend—The number you subtract.
difference—The answer in a subtraction problem.

Subtracting Two-Digit Numbers with Regrouping

What do you do when the digit in the ones place of the subtrahend is greater than the digit in the minuend? Add 10 to the smaller digit by taking 1 ten from the tens column. In subtraction, this is called regrouping.

Subtract: 21 − 7

tens   ones

Step 1: Are there enough ones in 21 from which to take 7? (*no*)

Step 2: Regroup 1 ten for 10 ones.

$$\begin{array}{r} {\scriptstyle 1\ \ 11} \\ 2\!\!\!/\,1\!\!\!/ \\ -\ 7 \\ \hline \end{array}$$

Step 3: Subtract ones.

$$\begin{array}{r} {\scriptstyle 1\ \ 11} \\ 2\!\!\!/\,1\!\!\!/ \\ -\ 7 \\ \hline 4 \end{array}$$

Step 4: Subtract tens.

$$\begin{array}{r} {\scriptstyle 1\ \ 11} \\ 2\!\!\!/\,1\!\!\!/ \\ -\ 7 \\ \hline 1\,4 \end{array}$$

21 − 7 = 14

Pretend you won a $99 shopping spree. Look in catalogs to determine what items you could purchase. Total the cost of the items and subtract it from $99. How close did you come to $99?

18. Subtracting Three-Digit Numbers

Did you know that blue whales have been known to live to the age of 100? People have been known to live to the age of 115. These numbers are three-digit whole numbers. Three-digit whole numbers consist of all the numbers from 100 through 999.

Subtracting Three-Digit Numbers without Regrouping

As you do when adding, arrange the numbers underneath each other. Always subtract from right to left. Subtract the ones column, then the tens column, and finally the hundreds column.

Subtract 785 − 642

Step 1: Arrange the numbers
underneath each other.

$$785$$
$$-642$$

Step 2: Subtract ones.

$$785$$
$$-642$$
$$3$$

Step 3: Subtract tens.

$$785$$
$$-642$$
$$43$$

Step 4: Subtract hundreds.

$$785$$
$$-642$$
$$143$$

$$785 - 642 = 143$$

Three-digit whole numbers are all the numbers from 100 through 999.

Subtracting Three-Digit Numbers with Regrouping

When subtracting two three-digit numbers with regrouping, use the following steps:

1. Arrange the numbers underneath each other.
2. If the ones digit in the subtrahend is greater than the ones digit in the minuend, then regroup 1 ten for 10 ones. If there are not enough tens, regroup 1 hundred for 10 tens. Subtract the ones.
3. If the tens digit in the subtrahend is greater than the tens digit in the minuend regroup one hundred for ten tens. Subtract the tens.
4. Subtract the hundreds.

Subtract 600 − 436

Step 1: Arrange the numbers underneath each other.

$$\begin{array}{r} 6\ 0\ 0 \\ -\ 4\ 3\ 6 \\ \hline \end{array}$$

Step 2: Regroup tens. Not enough tens. Regroup 1 hundred for 10 tens. Regroup 1 ten for 10 ones. Subtract ones.

$$\begin{array}{r} \overset{9}{5}\ \overset{\cancel{10}}{\cancel{10}}\ \cancel{10} \\ \cancel{6}\ \cancel{0}\ \cancel{0} \\ -\ 4\ 3\ 6 \\ \hline 4 \end{array}$$

Step 3: Subtract the tens.

$$\begin{array}{r} \overset{9}{5}\ \cancel{10}\ 10 \\ \cancel{6}\ \cancel{0}\ \cancel{0} \\ -\ 4\ 3\ 6 \\ \hline 6\ 4 \end{array}$$

Step 4: Subtract the hundreds.

$$\begin{array}{r} \overset{9}{5}\ \cancel{10}\ 10 \\ \cancel{6}\ \cancel{0}\ \cancel{0} \\ -\ 4\ 3\ 6 \\ \hline 1\ 6\ 4 \end{array}$$

Think of **regrouping** as another way to write a number.
600 is 6 hundreds. It is also 5 hundreds + 10 tens.

19. Subtracting Greater Numbers

Subtracting Greater Numbers without Regrouping

In subtraction without regrouping, the digits in the subtrahend are less than the digits in the minuend. Subtract from right to left, starting with the ones column.

Subtract 49,754 − 2,341

Step 1: Arrange the numbers underneath each other.

$$\begin{array}{r} 49,754 \\ -2,341 \end{array}$$ minuend
subtrahend

Step 2: Subtract ones.

$$\begin{array}{r} 49,754 \\ -2,341 \\ \hline 3 \end{array}$$

Step 3: Subtract tens.

$$\begin{array}{r} 49,754 \\ -2,341 \\ \hline 13 \end{array}$$

Step 4: Subtract hundreds.

$$\begin{array}{r} 49,754 \\ -2,341 \\ \hline 413 \end{array}$$

Step 5: Subtract thousands.

$$\begin{array}{r} 49,754 \\ -2,341 \\ \hline 7,413 \end{array}$$

Step 6: Subtract ten thousands.

$$\begin{array}{r} 49,754 \\ -2,341 \\ \hline 47,413 \end{array}$$ difference

$$49,754 - 2,341 = 47,413$$

greater numbers—Numbers with more than three digits.

Subtracting Greater Numbers with Regrouping

The New York Giants' stadium can seat 79,646 people. Arrowhead Stadium in Kansas City can seat 79,151. How many more people can be seated in Giant Stadium than in Arrowhead Stadium? To find the answer, you will have to use regrouping.

Find the difference in the seating capacity of the two stadiums. Subtract 79,646 − 79,151

Step 1: Arrange the numbers underneath each other.

$$\begin{array}{r} 79,646 \\ -79,151 \end{array}$$

Step 2: Subtract ones.

$$\begin{array}{r} 79,646 \\ -79,151 \\ \hline 5 \end{array}$$

Step 3: To subtract tens, regroup 1 hundred for 10 tens (10 + 4 = 14 tens).

$$\begin{array}{r} \overset{5\ \ 14}{79,\cancel{6}\cancel{4}6} \\ -79,151 \\ \hline 95 \end{array}$$

Step 4: Subtract hundreds.

$$\begin{array}{r} \overset{5\ \ 14}{79,\cancel{6}\cancel{4}6} \\ -79,151 \\ \hline 495 \end{array}$$

Step 5: Subtract thousands (9 − 9 = 0).

$$\begin{array}{r} \overset{5\ \ 14}{79,\cancel{6}\cancel{4}6} \\ -79,151 \\ \hline 495 \end{array}$$

Step 6: Subtract ten thousands (7 − 7 = 0).

There are 495 more seats at Giant Stadium than at Arrowhead Stadium.

Make up some subtraction word problems with a friend using greater numbers. It is a great way to practice subtraction of greater numbers.

20. Estimating Differences

Money, time, and distance can all be estimated. Estimation does not give you the exact answer. Rounding is often used to estimate differences.

If you did not already review page 16 to learn how to round whole numbers, you should do it now. Then come back to this page and continue with an example.

Rounding to the Greatest Place Value

A group of 538 runners started a long-distance race. There were 64 runners who did not finish the race. About how many runners completed the race? Estimate 538 − 64 to the greatest place value. The greatest place value is the hundreds place.

Step 1: Arrange each number according to place value.

$$538 \\ -64$$

Step 2: Round each number to the nearest hundreds.

538 **rounds to** 500
−64 **rounds to** −100

Step 3: Subtract.

$$500 \\ -100 \\ \hline 400$$

About 400 runners finished the race.

estimation—An opinion or judgment; a best guess.

Rounding to the Nearest Tens

Estimate again, this time rounding each number to the nearest tens.

Estimate 538 − 64

Step 1: Arrange each number
according to place value.

$$\begin{array}{r} 538 \\ -64 \end{array}$$

Step 2: Round each number to
the nearest tens.

538 **rounds to** 540
−64 **rounds to** −60

Step 3: Subtract ones.

$$\begin{array}{r} 5\ 4\ 0 \\ -\ 6\ 0 \\ \hline 0 \end{array}$$

Step 4: Subtract tens. Regroup
1 hundred for 10 tens
(10 tens + 4 tens = 14 tens).

$$\begin{array}{r} ^{4\ \ 14}\\ \cancel{5}\cancel{4}\ 0 \\ -\ 6\ 0 \\ \hline 8\ 0 \end{array}$$

Step 5: Subtract hundreds.

$$\begin{array}{r} ^{4\ \ 14}\\ \cancel{5}\cancel{4}\ 0 \\ -\ 6\ 0 \\ \hline 4\ 8\ 0 \end{array}$$

About 480 runners finished the race.

Estimation vs. Exact Difference

Find the exact difference:

$$\begin{array}{r} ^{4\ \ 13}\\ \cancel{5}\cancel{3}\ 8 \\ -\ 6\ 4 \\ \hline 4\ 7\ 4 \end{array}$$

Compare the exact difference with the differences you found when rounding.

Greatest Place Value	Rounding to Tens	Exact Difference
400	480	474

Rounding to the tens place is closer to the exact difference than rounding to the greatest place value.

Use your **estimation** skills to help someone do the weekly shopping. Estimate the total cost before going to the checkout. How close did you come to the actual price?

21. Subtraction Properties

As you read on page 18, there are three basic addition properties:

1. Commutative Property
2. Associative Property
3. Zero Property

Do these properties hold true for subtraction?

Commutative Property

The commutative property of addition allows you to add two numbers in any order you choose without affecting the sum. The sum of 7 plus 6 is the same as the sum of 6 plus 7.

$$\overset{?}{7 + 6 = 6 + 7}$$
$$13 = 13$$

Addition is commutative.

Is subtraction commutative? Use the same example. Is the difference of $7 - 6$ the same as the difference of $6 - 7$?

$$\overset{?}{7 - 6 = 6 - 7}$$
$$1 \neq {}^{-}1$$

The difference is not the same. One does not equal negative one. Order is important when you subtract numbers. You cannot subtract any two numbers in any way you choose.

> **Subtraction is not commutative.**

---

commute—To change places.
To review the **addition properties**, see pages 18 and 19.

Associative Property

Remember, the associative property of addition means that when you add three or more numbers, the way in which you group the numbers does not affect the sum.

Is the sum of (4 + 2) + 1 the same as the sum of 4 + (2 + 1)?

$$(4 + 2) + 1 = 4 + (2 + 1)$$
$$6 + 1 = 4 + 3$$
$$7 = 7$$

Is subtraction associative? Use the same example. Is the difference of (4 − 2) − 1 the same as the difference of 4 − (2 − 1)?

$$(4 - 2) - 1 \stackrel{?}{=} 4 - (2 - 1)$$
$$2 - 1 \stackrel{?}{=} 4 - 1$$
$$1 \neq 3$$

The difference is not the same. One does not equal three.

*Subtraction is **not** associative.*

The Zero Property

If you add zero to any number, the number remains the same.

$$4 + 0 = 4$$

Does the zero property hold true for subtraction?

$$4 - 0 = 4$$

If you subtract zero from any number, the number remains the same. Therefore, the zero property does hold true for subtraction.

Subtraction is neither commutative nor associative.

22. More Problem Solving

You have to make decisions every day. Deciding what you are going to wear or how much of your allowance you will spend each week is decision making. There are many ways to solve a problem. Understanding a problem is the first step.

The following steps are used to solve problems:

1. Find out what the problem asks for.
2. Choose a method, such as making an organized list, to solve the problem.
3. Find the answer to the problem.
4. Check the answer to see if it is reasonable.

Suppose you collect baseball cards and you have a total of 38 cards in your collection. You have 12 fewer National League baseball cards than American League cards. How many American League cards do you have? How many National League cards do you have?

Step 1: What do you have to find? The number of American League cards and the number of National League cards.

Step 2: Choose a method. Making an organized list is one strategy you can use to solve the problem.

Step 3: Find the answer.

One way to solve a problem is to make an organized list.

Make an organized list of all the family numbers of 38. Family numbers are all the combinations of two numbers that will give you a certain sum. You are trying to find two numbers that will give a sum of 38 and a difference of 12.

For your list, make the following columns: American League, National League, Sum, Difference, and Yes or No. Use the last column to answer whether you have a sum of 38 and a difference of 12.

American League	National League	Sum	Difference	Yes or No
38	0	$38 + 0 = 38$	$38 - 0 = 38$	No
37	1	$37 + 1 = 38$	$37 - 1 = 36$	No
36	2	$36 + 2 = 38$	$36 - 2 = 34$	No
35	3	$35 + 3 = 38$	$35 - 3 = 32$	No
34	4	$34 + 4 = 38$	$34 - 4 = 30$	No
33	5	$33 + 5 = 38$	$33 - 5 = 28$	No
32	6	$32 + 6 = 38$	$32 - 6 = 26$	No
31	7	$31 + 7 = 38$	$31 - 7 = 24$	No
30	8	$30 + 8 = 38$	$30 - 8 = 22$	No
29	9	$29 + 9 = 38$	$29 - 9 = 20$	No
28	10	$28 + 10 = 38$	$28 - 10 = 18$	No
27	11	$27 + 11 = 38$	$27 - 11 = 16$	No
26	12	$26 + 12 = 38$	$26 - 12 = 14$	No
25	**13**	**$25 + 13 = 38$**	**$25 - 13 = 12$**	**Yes**

You have 25 American League baseball cards and 13 National League baseball cards.

Step 4: Check the answer to see if it is reasonable. Is the sum of the American League and National League baseball cards equal to 38?
(*Yes:* $25 + 13 = 38$)
Are there 12 fewer National League baseball cards than American League baseball cards?
(*Yes:* $25 - 13 = 12$)

Do you collect baseball cards? How many National and American League cards do you have?

23. Subtracting Time Values

One of the basic mathematics needs of any society is a standard measurement of time. The calendar helps measure long periods of time. The clock helps measure short periods of time. There are 24 hours in one day but most clocks show twelve hours. The hands go around twice in 24 hours. Many ship and airline companies use a 24-hour clock to avoid confusion between A.M. and P.M.

Twelve-Hour Time and Twenty-Four-Hour Time

Write 7:30 A.M. using hours and minutes.

12-hour time: 7 hours 30 minutes
24-hour time: 0730

Write 3:45 P.M. using hours and minutes.

12-hour time: 3 hours 45 minutes
For 24-hour time, add 12 hours to P.M. hours.
24-hour time: 3 hours + 12 hours 45 minutes =
                15 hours 45 minutes
24-hour time: 1545

Subtracting Time Values without Regrouping

To subtract units of time, subtract the same units. Arrange them underneath each other. Subtract from right to left, starting with the smallest unit.

Calendars measure long periods of time. Clocks measure short periods of time.

Subtract 6 hours 55 minutes − 2 hours 20 minutes

Step 1: Subtract minutes.

$$\begin{array}{r} 6 \text{ hours } \mathbf{55 \text{ minutes}} \\ -2 \text{ hours } \mathbf{20 \text{ minutes}} \\ \hline \mathbf{35 \text{ minutes}} \end{array}$$

Step 2: Subtract hours.

$$\begin{array}{r} \mathbf{6 \text{ hours}} \text{ 55 minutes} \\ -\mathbf{2 \text{ hours}} \text{ 20 minutes} \\ \hline \mathbf{4 \text{ hours}} \text{ 35 minutes} \end{array}$$

Subtracting Time with Regrouping

Subtract 7 hours 18 minutes − 4 hours 45 minutes

Step 1: Regroup 1 hour for 60 minutes.

6 60 + 18 = 78

7 hours **18** minutes   minuend
−4 hours 45 minutes   subtrahend

Step 2: Subtract minutes.

6 78

7 hours **18 minutes**   minuend
−4 hours **45 minutes**   subtrahend
33 minutes

Step 3: Subtract hours.

6 78

7 hours 18 minutes   minuend
−**4 hours** 45 minutes   subtrahend
2 hours 33 minutes   difference

How many hours do you spend at school? What time do you arrive at school? What time are you dismissed?

How many hours a day do you sleep? What time do you go to sleep and what time do you wake up?

1 hour = 60 minutes

24. Subtracting Decimals

Decimals are used in science and industry. For example, modern balances used in science laboratories are digital, with the weight of an object recorded as a decimal.

Look at the place value of each digit in this number:

749.136

hundreds	tens	ones		tenths	hundredths	thousandths
7	4	9	.	1	3	6

The decimal point separates the whole number values to the left of the decimal point from the fractional parts to the right. The decimal point is placed between the ones and tenths places.

Subtracting Decimals without Regrouping

When you subtract decimal numerals, write them so that the decimal points are directly underneath one another. Subtract the numbers in the same way that whole numbers are subtracted. Place the decimal point in the answer directly underneath the decimal points in the problem.

Subtract 4.7 − 0.5

Step 1: Line up the decimal points.

$$\begin{array}{r} 4.7 \\ -0.5 \\ \hline \end{array}$$

Step 2: Subtract tenths. Place the decimal point in the difference.

$$\begin{array}{r} 4.7 \\ -0.5 \\ \hline .2 \end{array}$$

Step 3: Subtract ones.

$$\begin{array}{r} 4.7 \\ -0.5 \\ \hline 4.2 \end{array}$$

4.7 − 0.5 = 4.2

To **subtract decimals** with regrouping, line up the decimal points. Add zeros when necessary as placeholders.

Subtracting Decimals with Regrouping

Subtract 5.6 − 0.87

Step 1: Line up the decimal points. Add zeros as needed.

$$\begin{array}{r} 5\ .\ 6\ 0 \\ -0\ .\ 8\ 7 \\ \hline \end{array}$$

Step 2: Regroup 1 tenth for 10 hundredths. Subtract hundredths.

$$\begin{array}{r} {}^{5\ 10} \\ 5\ .\ \cancel{6}\ \cancel{0} \\ -0\ .\ 8\ 7 \\ \hline 3 \end{array}$$

Step 3: Regroup 1 one for 10 tenths (10 + 5 = 15 tenths). Subtract tenths.

$$\begin{array}{r} {}^{4\quad 15\ 10} \\ \cancel{5}\ .\ \cancel{6}\ \cancel{0} \\ -0\ .\ 8\ 7 \\ \hline 7\ 3 \end{array}$$

Step 4: Place the decimal point in the difference. Subtract ones.

$$\begin{array}{r} {}^{4\quad 15\ 10} \\ \cancel{5}\ .\ \cancel{6}\ \cancel{0} \\ -0\ .\ 8\ 7 \\ \hline 4\ .\ 7\ 3 \end{array}$$

I can do this!

In some countries a comma is used instead of a decimal point. For example, the number nine and seven tenths would be written as 9,7. We write this number as 9.7.

Find out which countries use which system. Are there other ways in which decimals are written?

When **subtracting decimals**, subtract the numerals as whole numbers. Place a decimal point in the difference directly below the decimal in the subtrahend.

25. Subtracting Monetary Values

Money is a part of everyday life. We see money amounts all around us, in newspapers, stores, and commercials, and on billboards and the Internet.

Money amounts are decimal numbers. Look at the following money amount: $3.47. The digits to the left of the decimal point are whole-dollar amounts. The whole-dollar amount for this example is three dollars. The digits to the right of the decimal point are fractional parts of a dollar amount. A cent is a hundredth of a dollar.

This figure shows 0.47 shaded.

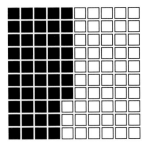

We read 0.47 as forty-seven cents. It also means forty-seven hundredths of a dollar. The digit to the immediate right of the decimal point is tenths of dollars. The four is four tenths of a dollar, or 40 cents.

This figure shows 0.40 shaded.

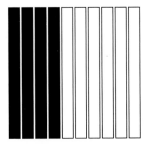

The next digit is hundredths of dollars. The seven is seven hundredths of a dollar, or 7 cents.

A cent is a hundredth of a dollar.

Monetary values are subtracted like other decimals.

Subtract $24.80 − $10.55

Step 1: Write the amounts over each other so that the decimal points line up.

$$\begin{array}{r} \$\ 2\ 4\ .\ 8\ 0 \\ -\$\ 1\ 0\ .\ 5\ 5 \end{array}$$

Step 2: Regroup tenths (1 tenth = 10 hundredths). Subtract hundredths.

$$\begin{array}{r} {}^{7\ \ 10} \\ \$\ 2\ 4\ .\ \cancel{8}\ \cancel{0} \\ -\$\ 1\ 0\ .\ 5\ 5 \\ \hline 5 \end{array}$$

Step 3: Subtract tenths. Place the decimal point in the difference.

$$\begin{array}{r} {}^{7\ \ 10} \\ \$\ 2\ 4\ .\ \cancel{8}\ \cancel{0} \\ -\$\ 1\ 0\ .\ 5\ 5 \\ \hline .\ 2\ 5 \end{array}$$

Step 4: Subtract ones. Subtract tens. Place the dollar sign in the difference.

$$\begin{array}{r} {}^{7\ \ 10} \\ \$\ 2\ 4\ .\ \cancel{8}\ \cancel{0} \\ -\$\ 1\ 0\ .\ 5\ 5 \\ \hline \$\ 1\ 4\ .\ 2\ 5 \end{array}$$

$24.80 − $10.55 = $14.25

You want to buy a video game and you have $20.00 to spend. Look at different advertisements to see where you can get the best bargain. What is the difference in prices between stores? How much can you save by choosing the best bargain?

Always remember to line up the decimal points.

26. Subtracting Integers

Integers are used in statistics, in science, and in stock market reports. Up to this point you have been adding and subtracting whole numbers, decimals, and fractions. Integers consist of the whole numbers and their opposites. The opposite of 4 is negative four (‾4). The opposite of 6 is negative six (‾6).

Subtracting Like Integers

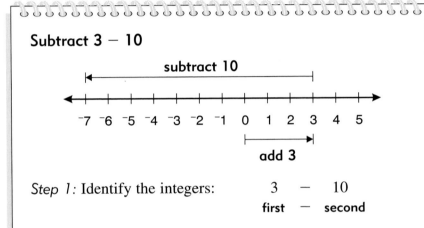

Subtract 3 − 10

Step 1: Identify the integers:

$$3 \quad - \quad 10$$
$$\textbf{first} \quad - \quad \textbf{second}$$

Step 2: Take the opposite sign of the second integer.

opposite of 10 is ‾10

Step 3: Change the operation of subtraction to addition.

$$3 + {}^-10$$

Step 4: Add the first integer to the second integer.

$$3 + {}^-10 = {}^-7$$

When adding integers with unlike signs, take the difference (10 − 3 = 7). Compare the two integers, ignoring the sign (10 > 3). Take the sign of the greater number (negative).

integers—All the whole numbers and their opposites (negatives).

. . . ‾5, ‾4, ‾3, ‾2, ‾1, 0, 1, 2, 3, 4, 5, . . .

Subtracting Unlike Integers

Subtract ⁻5 − 6

Step 1: Identify the integers.

$$⁻5 \quad - \quad 6$$
first — **second**

Step 2: Take the opposite sign of the second integer.

opposite of 6 is ⁻6

Step 3: Change subtraction to addition.

⁻5 + ⁻6

Step 4: Add. When adding like integers, add as whole numbers. The sign in the answer will be the original sign of the integers.

⁻5 + ⁻6 = ⁻11

Subtract 7 − ⁻8

Step 1: Identify the integers.

$$7 \quad - \quad ⁻8$$
first — **second**

Step 2: Take the opposite sign of the second integer.

opposite of ⁻8 is 8

Step 3: Change subtraction to addition.

7 + 8

Step 4: Add.

7 + 8 = 15

Record the highest and lowest temperatures for one week. What is the difference between them?

27. Subtracting Fractions

Look at a window. How is it divided? Is it divided into 4, 6, or 8 equal parts, or panes? Suppose your kitchen window is divided into 4 equal panes. One pane is $\frac{1}{4}$; 2 panes are $\frac{2}{4}$ or $\frac{1}{2}$; 3 panes are $\frac{3}{4}$; and 4 panes are $\frac{4}{4}$ or 1 window.

The term *fraction* comes from the Latin word *fractus*, meaning "broken." A fraction shows a relationship between a part and the whole item.

Subtracting Like Fractions

Like fractions are fractions with the same, or common, denominator.

Subtract $\frac{5}{8} - \frac{3}{8}$

Step 1: Subtract the numerators. Place the difference over the common denominator.

$$\frac{5-3}{8} = \frac{2}{8}$$

Step 2: Reduce the fraction to lowest terms by finding the greatest common factor (GCF) of the numerator and the denominator. To find the GCF of two numbers, follow these steps:

1. Find all the factors of the first number and all the factors of the second number.
2. Find the greatest common factor that appears in both numbers, and use this number to reduce the fraction.

factors of 2: 1, **2**

factors of 8: 1, **2**, 4, 8   GCF = 2

Step 3: Reduce by dividing the numerator and denominator by the GCF.

$$\frac{2 \div 2}{8 \div 2} = \frac{1}{4}$$

greatest common factor (GCF)—The largest number that will evenly divide into a set of numbers.

Subtracting Unlike Fractions

Unlike fractions are fractions with different denominators. To subtract unlike fractions, you need to change the fractions to like fractions with the same denominator.

Subtract $\dfrac{3}{4} - \dfrac{2}{3}$

Step 1: Find the least common denominator (LCD) by finding the least common multiple of the denominators.

multiples of 4: 4, 8, **12**, 16, . . .
multiples of 3: 3, 6, 9, **12**, 15, . . .   LCD = 12

Placing the least common multiple in the denominator of two fractions makes it the LCD.

Step 2: Write equivalent fractions using the LCD. How many 4s are there in 12? (*3*). Multiply numerator by 3 (3 × 3 = 9). How many 3s are there in 12? (*4*) Multiply numerator by 4 (2 × 4 = 8).

$$\frac{3}{4} = \frac{?}{12} = \frac{3 \times 3}{12} = \frac{9}{12}$$

$$\frac{2}{3} = \frac{?}{12} = \frac{2 \times 4}{12} = \frac{8}{12}$$

Step 3: Subtract.

$$\frac{9}{12} - \frac{8}{12} = \frac{9 - 8}{12} = \frac{1}{12}$$

With a friend, list all the places where you see fractions. Don't forget the gas station!

When you look at multiples of two numbers, the **common multiples** are in the sets of multiples for both numbers. The **least common multiple** is the smallest of these.

28. Subtracting Mixed Numbers

Did you know that in some countries students spend about three hours every day in music classes? What part of the student's day is spent in music class? Out of a 24-hour day, a student may spend $\frac{3}{24}$, or $\frac{1}{8}$, of the day in music class. These two fractions, $\frac{3}{24}$ and $\frac{1}{8}$, are called equivalent fractions. They have the same value.

You will need to find equivalent fractions when you are subtracting mixed numbers with unlike denominators.

Subtracting Mixed Numbers with Unlike Denominators

To subtract two mixed numbers with unlike denominators:

1. Rename the fractions so that they have a common denominator.
2. Subtract fractions from fractions and whole numbers from whole numbers.

Subtract $4\frac{1}{2} - 2\frac{1}{3}$

Step 1: Find the least common denominator (LCD).

multiples of 2:   2, 4, **6**, 8, . . .
multiples of 3:   3, **6**, 9, 12, . . .   LCD = 6

Step 2: Find equivalent fractions using the LCD. $\frac{1 \times 3}{2 \times 3} = \frac{3}{6}, \frac{1 \times 2}{3 \times 2} = \frac{2}{6}$

Step 3: Subtract fractions. $4\frac{3}{6}$

Subtract whole numbers. $-2\frac{2}{6}$

$2\frac{1}{6}$ **difference**

equivalent fractions—Fractions with equal values.
mixed number—A whole number and a fraction.

Subtracting Mixed Numbers with Regrouping

Sometimes the fraction in the first number is smaller than the fraction in the second number. You have to rename the fraction in the first number.

Subtract $3\frac{1}{5} - \frac{2}{5}$

Step 1: Rename the first mixed number. Subtract one from the whole number ($3 - 1 = 2$). The new numerator will be the sum of the old numerator and the denominator ($1 + 5 = 6$).

Rename $3\frac{1}{5}$

$3 - 1 = 2$

new numerator $= \dfrac{1 + 5}{5} = \dfrac{6}{5}$

So, $3\frac{1}{5} = 2\frac{6}{5}$

Step 2: Subtract numerators ($6 - 2 = 4$). Place the 4 over the denominator. Subtract whole numbers ($2 - 0 = 2$).

$$\begin{array}{r} 2\frac{6}{5} \\ -\ \frac{2}{5} \\ \hline 2\frac{4}{5} \end{array}$$

$$3\frac{1}{5} - \frac{2}{5} = 2\frac{4}{5}$$

That's cool.

Mixed numbers are often seen in recipes. With a friend or a family member, make your favorite dessert using a recipe from a cookbook. Find the difference of some of the ingredients in the recipe.

Further Reading

Books

Guthrie, Donna, and Jan Stiles. *Real World Math: Money, Credit, & Other Numbers in Your Life*. Brookfield, Conn.: Millbrook Press, 1998.

Maganzini, Christy. *Cool Math*. New York: Price Stern Sloan, 1997.

VanCleave, Janice P. *Janice VanCleave's Math for Every Kid: Easy Activities that Make Learning Math Fun*. New York: John Wiley & Sons, Inc., 1991.

Internet Addresses

CANITech. *Flashcards for Kids*. © 1999. <http://edu4kids.com/math/>.

Manura, David. *Dave's Math Tables*. © 1999. <http://www.jct.ac.il/scienceAndTechnology/Dave/>.

The Math Forum. *Ask Dr. Math*. © 1994–2000. <http://mathforum.org/dr.math>.

National Council of Teachers of Mathematics. *Figure This! Math Challenge for Families*. ©1999. <http://www.figurethis.org/index40.htm>.

Webmath. n.d. <http://www.webmath.com/index3.html>.

Index

N

negative integers, 28, 29, 56, 57

numerator, 30, 31, 32, 58, 61

O

one-digit numbers, 6–7, 36–37

P

partial sums, 15

placeholder, 25

place value, 14, 17

positive integers, 28, 29, 56, 57

problem solving, 20–21, 48

R

regrouping, 7, 9, 11, 13, 23, 24, 26, 27, 39, 41, 43, 45, 51, 53, 55, 61

rounding, 16, 44, 45

S

subtraction
of decimals, 52–53
of greater numbers, 42–43
of integers with like signs, 56
of integers with unlike signs, 57
of like fractions, 58
of mixed numbers, 60–61
of monetary values, 54–55
of one-digit numbers, 36–37
properties, 46–47
of three-digit numbers, 40–41
of time values, 50–51
of two-digit numbers, 38–39
of unlike fractions, 59

subtrahend, 38

T

terms, 9, 38

three-digit numbers, 12, 13, 40, 41

time values, 22–23, 50–51

two-digit numbers, 10, 11, 38, 39

U

unlike fractions, 30, 31, 59

unlike integers, 28, 29, 57

W

whole numbers, 6, 24, 28, 32, 33, 36, 60

Z

zero property, 19, 47